Machines  LB1

Tractors

Acknowledgments

Photographs: Pages 3, 10, 15, 17, 19, 23 and 24 © Massey Ferguson; pages 5 and 25 © Case; pages 7, 20 and 31 © Valtra; pages 9, 22, 29 and 37 © New Holland; page 12 © Lellovski77; page 16 © Dan Mighty Snail; page 27 © Robert Scarth; page 33 © Robin Thorn; page 35 © Peripitus.

Every effort has been made to contact copyright holders of material reproduced in this book. Any omissions will be rectified in subsequent printings if notice is given to the publishers.

Copyright © Axis Education 2012

All rights reserved; no part of this publication may be reproduced, stored in a retrieval system, transmitted in any form, or by any means, electronic, mechanical, photocopying, recording or otherwise, without the prior permission of the publisher.

Printed and bound in the UK by PublishPoint from KnowledgePoint Limited, Reading.

ISBN 978-1-84618-287-7

Axis Education
PO Box 459
Shrewsbury
SY4 4WZ

Email: enquiries@axiseducation.co.uk

www.axiseducation.co.uk

Tractors

A tractor is a farm machine. With a wide variety of attachments, it can be used for a huge number of jobs around the farm.

A Massey Ferguson pulling a trailer.

Machines at work

The word 'tractor' comes from the Latin 'trahere', meaning to pull. And that's exactly what it is designed to do – a tractor is a machine used on farms to pull tools.

The tractor may be slow, but it is a powerful machine that has allowed many farm jobs to be done by machine. Farmers use special attachments for ploughing, seeding, planting and all sorts of other tasks.

Modern tractors have on-board computers that can record its movements and repeat them with the touch of a button.

Tractors

A Case 370 double-wheeled tractor.

Machines at work

Tractors have big wheels with deep treads. This is to help the tractor keep grip, even in the thickest mud.

The front wheels of the tractor are smaller than the back wheels. They are used to steer the machine. Tractors can turn in a very tight circle.

In between the front wheels is a counterweight. This is a heavy piece of metal used to balance the weight at the back. The tractor would tip backwards without this extra weight.

Tractors

A Valtra tractor with the counterweight.

Farmers plough fields to cut and turn the soil so that it is ready to be planted. Ploughing buries any old surface plants and loosens the soil ready for seeds to be sown.

Machines at work

Before there were tractors, ploughs were pulled by horses. With today's tractors a farmer can work 30 times faster than a man with a horse.

The plough is attached to one of the hitches on the back of the tractor. The plough has mouldboards that turn over the soil. Each board cuts a furrow through the soil about 22 centimetres deep.

When the tractor reaches the end of the field, the driver lifts the plough out of the ground and turns it over. You can see the shiny mouldboards above and below the central beam of the plough.

Tractors

A New Holland tractor ploughing.

Machines at work

A harrow is a tractor attachment designed to break down clods of soil, uproot weeds, break up left over crops and to cover seed. Farmers may harrow a field if it has been left very uneven after ploughing.

Harrowing can be dusty work on a dry day.

There are different types of harrow. They almost always have a rigid frame with metal disks, teeth, or sharp points, called tines.

Some harrows have levers so the driver can alter how deeply it cuts. A harrow may have one or more gangs (sets) of cutting parts. Spike-tooth harrows have rigid teeth, while spring-tooth harrows have curved tines that adjust to obstacles – so are good for stony fields.

Machines at work

Rolling in the seed.

Once the farmer has ploughed the field she or he may need to roll it. Rolls are either flat metal rolls or a series of heavy rings. They are usually just over 6 metres wide. Farmers attach rolls to tractors for a couple of reasons. If harrowing has produced a very fine, blow-away soil, the roller helps to compact the soil so it doesn't blow away.

Rolling also helps crops in the early stages of growth. If a field is rolled right after seeds have been planted, the soil around the seed will compact which will keep it moist. This process gives the seed access to important nutrients.

Farmers sometimes roll crops, but only when the weather is dry. They lose some plants in the process, but rolling gets rid of slugs. Sometimes farmers add an extra set of wheels to the tractor to reduce the pressure it puts on the field.

Machines at work

A drill attachment sows seeds into rows in the soil, before covering them up. Farmers have to drill on the right day – both the weather and the soil help make that choice. Seeds must be sown at the right depth and then be covered up. If the ground is too wet or the soil is too lumpy, the drill won't work properly.

The hopper of the drill is a container that holds the seeds. Large hoppers can contain more than a tonne of seed. The right amount of seed must be drilled evenly across a field. If the seed rate is too high the crop will grow too closely together and may get disease. If the rate is too low, there may be bare patches that produce no crop at all. Drills have meters that control how much seed goes into the ground – the operator must alter the meter to suit each crop. A large fan blows the seeds down the pipes to reach across the width of the drill evenly.

The seeds then travel down the 'coulters'. These are metal tubes that cut a slot into the ground ready for the seed to land. Spring tines at the back of the coulters cover the seed up.

A Massey Ferguson with a large hopper.

Machines at work

Tractors are very versatile. With the right attachments farmers can also use them to spray their land.

Farmers usually spread two things on the land: pesticides and muck. Four main sorts of pesticide are used in the UK. Fungicides control disease, herbicides control weeds, insecticides kill insect pests and growth regulators stop plants becoming too tall.

Muck spreading – stand back!

Tractors

Spraying weed killer.

Machines at work

Farmers use tractors to cut and collect hay and straw. Straw is the dry stalks of plants that is used as bedding for animals. Hay is dried grass which is used for animal feed. The tractor pulls a mower that cuts the grass and leaves it in rows. These rows are known as swaths. Grass must be totally dry before it can be baled. The tractor pulls an attachment that turns the grass over so it can dry in the sun.

Farmers use a tractor with a baler attachment to pack hay and straw into bales. Bales are usually square or round. Round bales pack the hay more tightly and are wrapped in twine, net or plastic.

A Massey Ferguson with a round baler.

Modern balers can make fifty big bales an hour, before these machines were invented it could take a group of people days to harvest hay.

Machines at work

Moving feed using a Valtra tractor's loader bucket.

Often farmers need to scoop up materials to move them from one place to another. A tractor loader has a bucket at the front that the driver can move using a lever. The bucket is attached to an arm, known as the boom. The boom can bend in the middle to help the bucket move about and it can reach up high to move things.

The loader bucket can be taken on and off the tractor easily so that other attachments can be used. To move bales of hay or straw farmers can fix a bale fork to the front of the tractor. The bale fork spikes the bale then the driver raises the boom so that he or she can drive off.

Machines at work

Tractor attachments help farmers do all manner of jobs. Some of these jobs don't need to be done very often. To save money, a farmer may choose to hire an attachment instead of buying one.

Farmers dig ditches to help drain fields. A backhoe, a type of digging scoop, can be attached to a tractor to dig ditches.

A mini New Holland tractor digging a ditch.

Farmers use hedges and fences to divide their land. Tractor attachments can be used to look after hedges and fences. Hedge trimmers can be attached to a tractor to cut the tops and sides of hedges as the tractor drives along. A post driver is a tool that pushes fence posts into the ground. It acts like a hammer to bash the post down. Post drivers save hours of hard work.

Trimming the verge.

Machines at work

There are other tools to help farmers lift and shift things around the farm. There are attachments that turn a tractor into a forklift truck. You can get bag lifters, bale grabbers and spikes too.

Moving fertiliser with the help of a bag lifter.

Silage is a type of conserved grass that farmers make during the summer. It's used to feed cattle and sheep in winter. Animals prefer eating silage to hay. The tractor is an essential part of the process in silage making.

Firstly the tractor is used to mow the crop and leave it lying in swaths that are picked up with a forage harvester. The harvester picks up the grass and feeds it into a chopper. The chopped grass is dropped into a trailer.

Leaving the cut grass ready to be harvested.

In the farm yard the grass is dropped in a heap called a clamp. Farmers need to make sure that the clamp is in a place that is easy to get to during the winter. To build the clamp they have to get as much air out of the grass as possible. To do this the tractor drives over the clamp again and again until it is compact enough to walk on.

The silage clamp is covered with black plastic sheeting making sure it is airtight. Then the farmer puts hundreds of tyres on top to help it stay airtight ready to feed animals over the winter.

Tractors

Making the clamp.

Machines at work

If land is very muddy or wet, farmers may use a tractor with crawler tracks. A crawler tractor moves on tracks instead of wheels. The purpose of the track is to spread the tractor's weight over a larger surface area so that the tractor doesn't squash the ground too much. This allows the tractor to move safely over wet ground such as muddy fields or snow.

The ridges on the rubber tracks are called lugs. You can see from the photo that there is a mechanism within the track that helps the machine move. The crawler tractor was the basis of the first designs of military tanks.

Tractors

A crawler tractor working through the night.

Machines at work

Gone are the days when tractor drivers bounced around in loud tractor cabs all day long. Tractor driving used to be very hard on the body. Modern tractors give drivers a pleasant place to work. Just like the latest cars, they even come with cup holders and wide seats.

New tractors have quiet and comfortable cabs. They have plenty of space, easy-to-use monitors and controls and great visibility. Many tractors have seats that can be angled and controlled for total driver comfort.

Tractors

The cockpit of a Valtra tractor – with all mod cons.

Machines at work

Changing a tractor tyre is just like changing the tyre on a car, but because of the size of the vehicle, it's not an easy job. You need more than one person to help. The most important thing is safety. You need to make sure the tractor is parked on even ground. The front and rear wheels need to be blocked. Then, just as you would with a car, you can raise the tractor with a heavy-duty jack and support.

Make sure the tractor can't roll forward, backward or side to side before you start to remove the wheel nuts and get on with swapping over the tyre. These workers have removed a tyre from a John Deere 7520 tractor which has double back wheels.

Tractors

Changing a tractor tyre is often a team effort!

Machines at work

Tractor pulling is a sport that's not just for farmers. Tractor pulling is all about finding the strongest machine and the best driver. It's quite different to all other motorsports because it's not about being the fastest. Tractor pulling bills itself as the world's most powerful motorsport.

One by one, machines compete to pull a sled as far down a track as possible. The aim is to pull the sled along the entire length of the 100m track. But the further the tractor pulls the sled, the harder it is to tow. Whoever pulls the sled the furthest wins.

There are dozens of classes, depending on the size of the tractor. Class sizes vary from 8 horsepower lawn mower tractors to massive 12,000 horsepower modified tractors.

Tractors

The world's most powerful motorsport?

Machines at work

Tractor drivers usually wear overalls to work. Whatever you wear, you need to make sure that your clothes aren't loose and likely to get caught in the machinery. John has been driving a tractor on a big farm in Suffolk since he left school five years ago.

"I always give the tractor a quick once over before I set out – things like tyre pressure and oil should be looked at, as you don't want to break down."

"If the tractor has been used by another driver I'll adjust the seat so I can use the controls properly. The sorts of jobs I do each day will depend on the time of year. In the spring I do a lot of ploughing and harrowing. The farm I work on has huge fields. I listen to my iPod or the radio during the day. At lunchtime I usually arrange to meet one of the other drivers and we'll sit and eat our lunch together."

"When I'm about to finish for the day, I slow the tractor to a gradual stop to let the engine cool as the machinery gets very hot after heavy work."

Tractors

Fuelling the tank ready for a day in the field.

Machines at work

Technical specification – Massey Ferguson MF8690

This is Massey Ferguson's biggest and most powerful tractor ever.

Power	340 horsepower
Engine	8.4 litre 6 cylinder diesel
Field speed range	0-17mph forward, 0-10mph reverse
Road speed range	0-31mph forward, 0-24mph reverse
Gears	Infinitely variable forward and reverse in 2-7mph range
Hitch lift capacity	10,823kg
Turning circle	13.2 metres
Fuel tank capacity	630 litres
Wheelbase	3.1 metres
Weight	10,300kg
Tyres	Front 600/65R34 Rear 710/75R42
Height to top of cab	3.38 metres
Price	£156,070

Technical specification – Massey Ferguson MF1520A

Small in size but high in performance, the MF1520A is Massey Ferguson's smallest tractor.

Power	19.5 horsepower
Engine	8.4 litre 3 cylinder diesel
Speed range	0–19.5mph forward, 0–22.8mph reverse
Gears	8 forward and 8 reverse
Hitch lift capacity	600kg
Fuel tank capacity	28 litres
Wheelbase	1.56 metres
Weight	840kg
Tyres	Front: 6.06.00-12 Rear: 9.5-160-12
Height to top of cab	2.01 metres
Price	£12,000

Glossary

attachments	extra parts that can be added to a piece of equipment
counterweight	a weight that is as heavy as something else, so that the two objects can balance
forage harvester	a large machine for harvesting grass or hay
horsepower/hp	a unit for measuring the power of an engine
mouldboards	a board on a plough that turns the earth over
obstacles	objects which block your way, so that you must try to go around them
nutrients	chemicals or food that provides what is needed for plants or animals to live and grow
versatile	having many uses
pesticides	chemical substances used to kill insects and small animals that destroy crops
visibility	how far or how well you can see